AMERICAN ARCHITECTURE

american architecture

THOMAS H. CREIGHTON

Illustrated by PAUL SPREIREGEN

ROBERT B. LUCE, INC. WASHINGTON, D.C.

AMERICA TODAY Series, No. 1

AMERICAN ARCHITECTURE

© Copyright 1964 by ROBERT B. LUCE, INC.

Library of Congress Catalog Card Number: 64-19598

Manufactured in the United States of America

WESTERN PRINTING AND LITHOGRAPHING COMPANY
Cambridge, Maryland

Cover Design by STEPHEN KRAFT

TABLE OF CONTENTS

PART I

THE GROWTH OF AMERICAN ARCHITECTURE

INTRODUCTION

Architecture is the most visible symbol of a society. What man builds to shelter his personal and social activities expresses the nature of those activities, his political, emotional, and esthetic attitudes, the abundance or poverty of his economy, and the tools and techniques that he has developed. However, one cannot view the monuments of past civilizations superficially, if one hopes to gain a deeper insight into the lives of the people of those times. Nor can one jump to conclusions about the United States of America in the twentieth century by a quick look at a few buildings by Frank Lloyd Wright, or, on the other hand, at a few ugly and ill-planned subdivisions.

In order to understand the great variety of buildings and the wide diversity of architectural expression in the United States today, one must look more closely at our architecture than the usual person who passes by these buildings might do.

What, for example, do the thousands of new schools tell us about attitudes toward education in the United States—or, indeed, toward family life, the arts and sciences, or social aims in general?

What do the forms of concrete structures, the design of glass-walled buildings, the arrangement of semi-prefabricated housing developments, tell us about the technical knowledge and construction skills that have developed in the American building industry?

What understanding of the country can we gain from analyzing the reasons for architects' choices among the many building materials and methods available today?

The task of trying to evaluate, of even attempting to see deeply into, contemporary architecture in the United States is not as easy as it was in other times. American architecture is a product of previous building in other countries, especially in Europe. In some ways, it shows clear, new directions, and in other ways it is a remarkable combination of diverse theories, concepts, and technologies. We could say that it expresses an affluent society, extravagant in the volume and the quality of its building—and we would be partially right. Or we could say that too many buildings are restricted by budget and tend to ignore nuances of design and the sister arts of sculpture and painting —and again we would be partially right. We could comment that American technology is extremely advanced in the use of factory-made parts; or we could correctly note that building technology lags behind that of other industrial activities in the United States. It would be equally true to remark that recent American architecture has influenced work in almost every country of the world, and, on the other hand, that the inspiration for much of what is being done here was originally derived from foreign influences.

It is the purpose of this book to indicate what some of those influences have been, what the native developments have contributed, what the present expression is, and what effect architecture in America today may have on future trends both at home and in other countries where its influence is so rapidly extending.

1.

COLONIAL BUILDING

In the very beginnings of its Colonial period (1630-1770), architecture in America naturally was patterned after buildings in the original countries of its European settlers. Yet, from the very start of colonization, the country's architecture began to adapt itself to the terrain, climate, and materials available.

The earlier architecture on the North American continent—that of the successive Indian civilizations—has been largely ignored even to the present time, with the exception of a few cave dwellings that are monumental historic curiosities. The adobe construction of the Indian *pueblos* has influenced design in some southwest areas of the country, but usually in a superficial manner.

Certainly the contact of the early colonists with the Indians was not on a level of cultural exchange. It forced them, indeed, to build solid, protective buildings as safe as possible from attack. Heavy timber construction of a late medieval nature, such as the early Americans remembered from Europe, was appropriate and practical; a construction system of interlocking wooden sills, posts, beams, and rafters soon became common along the east coast settlements. The remembered stucco or brick infills between the posts of "half-timber" construction in Europe were replaced, however, by wood surfacing inside and out. The original one- or two-room house, with a single chimney and a single shed roof, expanded into a multi-room, story-and-a half- or two-story building, with two or more chimneys, with a central hall, and with pitched roofs that might bear more than one gable. Then the structure and the wood surfacing became more sophisticated. Posts and beams were more accurately sized, and more carefully finished. As time went on, Renaissance and classic detail was added to the exterior, and door and window proportions were thoughtfully studied. Interiors finally received equally solicitous design attention. The results however, were almost always homespun; the "formal" styles of Europe lost precision, but gained a direct sort of naïve vigor.

In those days, of course, there was a time lag in receiving concepts from outside the country. Early Colonial work was in many ways similar to the vestiges of the late middle ages in Europe—for example, there was influence from the English period known as Tudor. "Bacon's Castle," a house built in Virginia in the third quarter of the seventeenth century, and a nearby brick church with "Gothic" detail, are interesting instances. The successive Renaissance periods of England and France in their turn influenced the colonies and the new states with a lag of perhaps half a century. And if the European prototypes seemed to be misunderstood, misinterpreted, or distorted, it was partially because of awkward communications, but more often because the local situation required indigenous changes that were freely and ingeniously made. One interesting example is the New England meeting house. Designed and built literally as a house, rectangular and with pitched roofs, it had little relationship to any previous religious edifice, and it established its own style with additions and changes of superficial detail, and with towers and porches added at various times. This style has persisted through many periods of development in religious architecture in America.

As a historical study, the local and regional variations within the architecture of the Colonial period are fascinating. But they contribute little to an understanding of today's architectural expression.

At first, of course, there were English-influenced buildings along the East Coast, French-inspired structures in some southern territories, Spanish styles that fused with Indian building methods in the Southwest. These were the strong backgrounds, and many of these buildings remain, or at least have been well photographed. (The United States has never been very conscientious about preserving examples of its architectural history.) There were other, sometimes extremely interesting variations on the original European themes, such as the German "Pennsylvania Dutch" buildings with rugged stone walls and heavy timber gambrel roofs. But it was the English influence that became dominant through various Renaissance styles brought from that home country: the "pure" Renaissance, architecture adapted from the Italian Renaissance architect Palladio, and then the personal interpretations of the English architects Inigo Jones and Christopher Wren. These styles, fused with

Mission of San Juan Capistrano, California
Architect UNKNOWN

anonymous, indigenous expressions in America, produced the characteristic work of the eighteenth century. Buildings in the settlements and the growing cities along the East Coast, from New York to Virginia (where Williamsburg, a carefully restored town of that period, is the well-known example) settled into what became known later as the Georgian style, with many variations but with a character sufficiently refined to make it a recognizable and very pleasant stage in architectural history.

Although American architecture has been marked from the first by a synthesis of influences from many sources, it has been defined equally by a continual progression toward a greater national similarity of expression. Some critics even today deplore the disappearance of regional differences. For reasons that will be discussed later, the few continuing local dissimilarities have become less and less important and even the strong original variations due to varied origins of the colonists began to fuse quickly into a Colonial Style.

THE ARCHITECTURE OF THE YOUNG STATES

The formal record of architecture in the new United States, during the half century after the conclusion of the Revolutionary War, is usually a listing of derivative stylistic periods. There was a period of Greek Revivalism, and there was a period of Gothic Revivalism, each with its talented practitioners. There was a continuing Palladian Renaissance attitude, championed and demonstrated by Thomas Jefferson, American statesman and architect, in the buildings he designed for the University of Virginia. But there was also the very original work of Benjamin Latrobe and of Charles Bulfinch, the first two formally trained architects in the United States.

During this time the city of Washington, D.C., had its architectural beginnings, with the inception of its grand axial plan conceived by Pierre Charles L'Enfant, a French engineer. The construction of the President's home, the White House, marked the beginning of a residential area around what is now Lafayette Square. The National Capitol (the design of which was selected as a result of a national competition) was started by Dr. William Thornton, modified by Stephen Hallet, domed by Latrobe, and finally unified to a large degree by Bulfinch.

Toward the middle of the nineteenth century there began the first wave of eclecticism in the States—that is, a free borrowing and use of architecture from any (or many) previous historical eras.

Through all of these pigeonholed and overlapping "periods" (Greek Revival, 1820-1850; Gothic Revival, 1830-1860; etc.) there run many individual variations. There were romanticists such as Richard Upjohn, architect of Trinity Church in New York; technical innovators like Charles Bogardus, who built

8

an early cast iron factory; and purists like Horatio Greenough, the sculptor, who demanded "the immediate banishment of all make-believe." And there also persisted the development of a characteristic building form that was to spread through the country for many generations—a rectangular form, with its structure made up of posts that supported beams and girders, covered with wood siding in most cases, with windows symmetrically arranged, and with a pitched roof. It was basically a classic form, no matter from what source the ornament might be derived; its native origin was quite clearly the New England dwelling.

As the country expanded to the west, this generic building type, used for houses, churches, stores, schools, and even jails, was carried through Ohio (where much architecture in the northern part of the state was almost directly transplanted from New England), to the opening Midwest, and even to California and Oregon during the Gold Rush.

It is necessary to remember that a large part of this construction, outside the comparatively few examples by those who considered themselves professional architects, was anonymous. It was built by homesteaders themselves or by builders with little or no formal training. The simple, easily erected structural system was the important element in "design," and the "architecture" might be added by using a handbook of ornament, or by buying scrollwork and mouldings that could be applied by the yard. Thus much of the architecture of the expanding States was utilitarian in nature, and achieved what style it had quite accidentally. This is, of course, the natural way for an architectural style to grow. When more important buildings, usually in masonry rather than wood, began to be added to the environment of the growing towns across the country, this same application of copied and often little understood ornamental detail produced some very interesting, sometimes awkward, but often appealing city halls, churches, and large town houses. Even the Greek Revival, which rapidly became almost a national "style," was in many cases simply a columned porch and a pediment added to the basic rectangular form. Its original purity was soon absorbed into local mannerisms and methods of building.

This same emphasis on simplicity of building method, and lack of concern with formal esthetics of design, is apparent in the development of the balloon frame and the simple salt-box house that expressed it in the Midwest of the 1830's. The balloon frame is a light wood structural-frame system, covered (and thereby braced) with wood boards. A thinner, cheaper, braced version of the New England wood post construction, it depended for its connections on nails rather than on the earlier tongued wood joints. It has persisted to this day, as the typical builder's method of quick and easy construction, defying prefabricated factory methods. It produces a box-like building that has neither long life nor great beauty. But it has made it possible for more people than one would expect, in an industrialized society, to own their own homes. The architectural and planning problem that this comparatively early development in American building still poses to today's professionals will be discussed later.

Nevertheless, while the original simple New England structure was spreading across the country, the development of more formal styles continued in the big cities. And inevitably, as time went on, more Americans chose architecture as a career, and the profession itself became more formalized and better organized. Soon American architects were going to Paris, to l'Ecole des Beaux Arts, for their training. In 1866 the Massachusetts Institute of Technology established an independent course in architecture in the States—the first college to do so.

3.

THE SEARCH FOR A STYLE

The maturing of architecture in the United States truly did not begin until after the Civil War. From that point on, there was evident, both in the design of buildings and the literature about the design, a strong desire to find an idiom that would express the particular culture of the developing States. There was evident the wish to develop a way of building that would be related to the growing industrial power of the country. In addition, there were moves to improve the quality both of the product itself—the building and the city in which the building was erected—and of the production process, which in architecture means the development and practice of a true, organized profession. The American Institute of Architects was founded in 1857 for the express purpose of elevating the profession. Other schools of architecture followed the early lead of M.I.T. and offered professional courses. But within this growing development of American architecture at least two distinct, markedly different attitudes became apparent.

First, there was a strong movement on the East Coast, led by the extremely capable firm of McKim, Mead & White, toward further adaptation of earlier work (sometimes from classical Rome, sometimes from the Renaissance periods) to the contemporary U.S. scene. Theirs was a different attitude, however, from the blind copying of lesser architects. Their mastery of detail was precise, tasteful, and understanding. Within some of the buildings they created (such as the Pennsylvania Railroad Station in New York) there was a sense of space that has seldom been achieved since; their façades, not always related to these interior spaces, were bold and knowing adaptations of the borrowed antecedents. Unfortunately, their followers and colleagues were seldom as capable or as disciplined.

The second stream of work in the last half of the nineteenth century might also be said to have started from a bold adaptation of traditional mannerisms, but it very soon became much more than that. First there was a move toward simplification of form and design. Henry Hobson Richardson, one of the truly great architects of the United States, who had a prolific practice in the 1870's and the 1880's, cut boldly through the academic attitudes of the time. Starting with a somewhat Romanesque sense of simple forms, he soon became strong and original in his handling of masses. In his work, details and even ornamental and textural surfacing were closely related to and inte-

Marshall Field Wholesale Warehouse, Chicago, Illinois
Architect: HENRY HOBSON RICHARDSON

grated with the forms themselves, rather than applied. If his Trinity Church in Boston, Massachusetts, still seemed somewhat derivative, his Marshall Field Wholesale Store in Chicago, Illinois, was one of the first large commercial buildings to express in rational and dignified terms a new building type that was becoming increasingly important.

Richardson, then, provided an inspirational direction in the esthetics of architecture—markedly different from the work of his former assistants, Charles Follin McKim and Stanford White. At the same time certain technical and economic reasons encouraged the development of a new approach. As land in the major cities—notably New York and Chicago—grew more expensive and was more intensively used, it became obviously desirable to build higher, especially for commercial purposes. And as the urge to build "skyscrapers" increased, the materials for doing so became more available. There had been for some time experiments in the use of cast iron, the forerunner of steel and metal frame construction. In the 1850's the first rather crude, hydraulically operated elevators were used in New York.

The story of the beginning of the modern high-rise office building, using a skeleton frame of metal rather than depending on the bearing qualities of a thick masonry wall, is an interesting one. After early experiments in New York, the scene shifted to Chicago, where architects such as Daniel H. Burnham, John W. Root, William LeBaron Jenney, and Louis H. Sullivan and his engineer partner, Dankmar Adler, made successive advances in the new idiom. Their contributions were in esthetics, and also in engineering and construction techniques; and the fusion of these two aspects of architecture marked the beginnings of what might have become in time a strong American style. The earlier buildings of this Chicago "school"—even those by Sullivan, the strongest and most influential of the group—used few of the new technical possibilities. The search then was for verticality of expression that would be valid for a building of greater height than had previously been attained in our time. A sense of modulation (the repetition of a regular spacing) in the treatment of windows and piers that would indicate the repetitive nature of the offices within the building was also sought. But soon, in skyscraper office buildings in Chicago, there was a use of metal frame on the upper floors, with the lower stories still of wall-bearing masonry, as in Jenney's Home Life Insurance Building. There appeared also a use of spread foundations—a sort of raft, floating on the muddy subsoil—as in Burnham & Root's Montauk Building. And finally, there was used a terra-cotta surfacing over a complete metal frame, as in Burnham & Root's Reliance Building, and Adler and Sullivan's Wainwright Building, with none of the ornamentation that was used in earlier periods of U.S. architectural history.

The contribution that these men made to architecture, not only in the United States but in all parts of the world where formal, architect-designed building was taking place, was very great. And yet one must remember the limitations of their new-found design freedom. Sullivan was a prolific writer, and his diatribes against the meaningless copying of Roman temples for midwest bank buildings, for instance, make good lusty reading today. Nevertheless, in an essay on the esthetics of the high-rise building, and in the work that he accomplished in this category, he was still sufficiently disciplined in the classic values to insist that a skyscraper must have a distinct base, shaft and cornice. In some of his later tall buildings the transition between these parts of the building became less marked and the elements themselves—notably the cornice and the vertical piers between windows on the shaft—simpler and more directly handled.

Sullivan, as an individual, must be remembered for more than his part in skyscraper development. Toward the end of his

Wainwright Building, St. Louis, Missouri
Architect: LOUIS SULLIVAN

life, (which terminated in a tragically declining practice and an ever greater isolation from society) he built a number of banks, some quite small, throughout the midwestern states. In these buildings, more than in any others, one can see his system of ornament—original, controlled, foliated, rich. In some of the buildings the ornament almost dominates the basic architectural form, but always, whether cast in terra cotta for use on a building, or simply drawn as an illustration for one of the many plates he completed, it remains one of the very few successful attempts in modern times to find a decorative art form that is architectural in character and not derivative in expression.

The influence of Sullivan inevitably spread in the Chicago area. Younger architects who had been trained in his office left to start their own practices and his mark remained on their work. The best known of these apprentices was Frank

National Farmer's Bank, Owatonna, Minnesota
Architect: LOUIS SULLIVAN

Lloyd Wright, who, despite many difficulties with Sullivan, remained loyal to him throughout his life and appreciative of the work of the older man.

The Columbian Exposition of 1893 in Chicago marked the end of this Chicago period of development in architecture in the United States, and it is the work of Wright after that time that is the continuing thread which leads through an almost fifty year gap in creative design which resulted from the architecture of that World's Fair. There were two strong bids for the design of the principal buildings in the Exposition: one from the group of architects on the East Coast who were dominated by McKim, Mead & White; and another from the developing Chicago group led by Burnham & Root and illustrated best by Sullivan. The white classic attitude of the Easterners won out, and the pompous temporary structures that millions of Americans saw on the fair grounds—beautifully landscaped in formal patterns and reflected in romantic lagoons—influenced for a long while those who commissioned design in the United States. Sullivan's very striking Transportation Building, one of the few non-classical pavilions, was admired by architectural critics but considered by the visitors to be more an interesting oddity than a serious architectural statement.

Thus it was that the beginnings of an original American design philosophy in the Chicago school were cut short, not to be remembered and carried further until a half century later. And by the time a new wide search for an architecture expressing our own era began, both the technological developments (materials to build with, mechanical equipment to service the buildings) and esthetic philosophies (mainly reflections of the early modern movements in Europe) had moved beyond the comparatively naïve beginnings in Chicago. But Frank Lloyd Wright, in his work and in his writings provided a link with those beginnings and the twentieth century.

Wright's first work as an architect on his own, after he left
Sullivan's office, was a series of homes that have become known
as the "prairie houses." Even in this early work he indicated his
great contribution: the ability to arrange interior spaces so that
they provide interesting, often contrasting relationships to one
another, yet remain unified and count as one consolidated space.
In the other work he did in his first decade of practice—particularly the Larkin Administration Building in Buffalo, N.Y.,
and a Unitarian church in Illinois known as Unity Church—
this ability to mold and sculpture space became even more evident. The Larkin Building (now destroyed) was a great inner,
sky-lighted space with galleries of offices supported on bold
interior piers. Unity Church, which was basically a great auditorium, achieves a feeling of intriguingly subdivided space by

Transportation Building, Chicago, Illinois
Architect: LOUIS SULLIVAN

in-cut corners and double banks of galleries on three sides.

Wright's later work is divided into two active periods—that up to 1920, during which he designed Midway Gardens, a recreation place in Chicago, the Imperial Hotel in Tokyo, and some other, often highly decorated structures; and then, after a hiatus, a later time of production beginning in the late 1930's. Wright spent a large part of his life ignored by his fellow architects in the United States, and completely unknown by the general public. There was much that was negative in Wright's attitudes and much that looked back to the lusty nineteenth century romanticism of Walt Whitman. Wright hated cities; he had contempt for most architects; his concern with function was minor; his interest in technology was nominal. What was positive was personal, an expression of his great genius as a

Unity Church, Oak Park, Illinois
Architect: FRANK LLOYD WRIGHT

creative artist; it could not very well be copied, except as tricks and clichés, nor taught, except as wordy dogmatism. There is, unhappily, an almost negligible influence of his work on other

Johnson's Wax Company, Racine, Wisconsin
Architect: FRANK LLOYD WRIGHT

architects only a few years after his death. To say this is not
in any sense to detract from his great contribution at the turn
of the century and in the years following, during his lonely,
bitter struggle for those principles that in the end he resented
seeing others carry forward.

During the bad times at home, however, Wright's reputa-
tion spread around the world through publication of his work.

In the later period he designed the famous house for the
Kaufmann family in Pennsylvania, "Falling Water," the administration building for the Johnson's Wax Company in Racine,
Wisconsin, and a college in Florida. In these and other commissions he showed an interest in many materials, in numerous
structural forms, and in further manipulation of interior space.

In his latest work, culminating in the Guggenheim Museum
in New York, Wright seemed largely concerned with development of stylistic expressions of his own personality—ramps,
overhangs, extended horizontal lines, cut-off corners, and so on
—although his ability to do remarkable things with space always remained, as the curved, sky-lighted interior of the Guggenheim Museum indicates.

In the meantime, even through the new period of classical
copyism that followed the postponed promise of the Chicago
school, there were some architects of talent (many of whom
have only recently been appreciated) who found design inspiration in the work of neither the eastern nor midwestern schools,
but searched elsewhere for forms they thought appropriate.
Stemming partly from Richardson, work developed in the
"shingle style"—quite open planning, informal arrangement of
shapes and forms, asymmetrical grouping of windows and
door openings, informal porches; it also was ultimately stifled in
the 1890's by the revivalist fashion popularized by McKim,
Mead & White.

One of the most important concentrations of original ability was in California. There, in the period just after the turn of the century, Bernard R. Maybeck, the Greene Brothers (Charles S. and Henry M.), Irving Gill, and several other unusually talented architects did highly individual work with a regional flavor, a sense of the local topography and climate, and a knowledgeable use of local materials such as redwood. Maybeck, the most gifted if not the most consistent one of the group, has left a number of very bold structures—for example the Christian Science Church in Berkeley, California—that combine a rugged use of wood with other materials, even such a universal one as concrete.

This West Coast work possessed an almost oriental sense of dignified relationship with the landscape. And in the projecting eaves, carved rafter ends, and wide expanses of glass that

First Church of Christ Scientist, Berkeley, California
Architect: BERNARD MAYBECK

allowed the often-present view to be seen, there were again the beginnings of a distinct style. But as in Chicago, the advance in California was stifled by the influence of exposition architecture. Like the Columbian Exposition in Chicago, the Panama-Pacific Exposition in San Francisco and the San Diego Exposition, both in 1915, were designed with great formality as artificial classical cities, and the public that came to the expositions seemed to like what they saw better than their own regional architecture. Maybeck, like Sullivan, designed an exposition building, but unlike Sullivan's Transportation Building in Chicago, Maybeck's Palace of Fine Arts in San Francisco (still being preserved at great cost by that city) was a fantasy in romantic classicism. Maybeck lived on and continued to do work until 1957 (at his death he was ninety-five years old), but his influence never extended beyond his own region.

4.

THE QUIET ADVANCE

Unless one searches below the surface, it appears that except for the work of a few individuals in isolated places the first quarter of the twentieth century saw no advance and very little study leading toward a contemporary United States architecture. Although a large volume of building was put in place, even the most ardent patriot has to admit that nothing of any great design importance, and much of extremely bad taste, was accomplished prior to and through the boom years of the 1920's and into the depression years of the 1930's. McKim, Mead & White continued to be a dominant firm for some decades, but the quality of their design gradually decreased. A new sort of arbitrary choice of design set in, with certain styles deemed appropriate for certain types of buildings. Ralph Adams Cram developed a Gothic imitation for churches, and his one-time partner Bertram Grosvenor Goodhue rivaled it with a Byzantine adaptation that he even used, in modernized versions, for other buildings such as the State Capitol in Lincoln, Nebraska. Classic Roman was the architecture for banks, and collegiate Gothic was popular for school and college buildings. In fact, Gothic motifs, notable for spires and pointed arches, were the common means of striving for verticality in skyscrapers, now that the studies of the Chicago school were forgotten. Cass Gilbert's Woolworth Building in New York and Hood & Howell's Chicago Tribune Tower in Chicago were looked on as masterpieces of the effort. Many new buildings were put up in Washington, D.C. during the 1930's, most of which demonstrated the ba-

Chicago Tribune Building, Chicago, Illinois
Architect: RAYMOND M. HOOD
& JOHN MEADE HOWELLS

nality and the functional malfeasance of stately stylism.

Influences from outside the country continued, but unfortunately were not salutary ones. *L'Ecole des Beaux Arts* in Paris remained the mecca of most American architects, and the Paris Prize, a sort of scholarship allowing study there, was the goal of American architectural students. This school taught a romanticized classical design, characterized by symmetrical, regular arrangement of building elements along major and minor axes. Important points in the plan were emphasized by heavy piers, and accents were provided in the elevations by sculptured figures, urns, or other somewhat altered classic features. These *Beaux Arts* hallmarks exerted a strong influence on both architectural work and education for architecture in the U.S. More schools of architecture were being founded, and just as Harvard, Princeton, M.I.T. and the other large eastern schools called prominent French *Beaux Arts* teachers to head their design departments, the newer and smaller schools brought to their faculties French architects of lesser talents.

The extravagant building boom of the 1920's, followed by the stock market crash in the fall of 1929, marked the end of this quantitatively large but qualitatively inferior period in American architectural history. The boom had provided too many buildings, and architectural activity very nearly stopped for some years. The years of the great depression of the 1930's appeared, for this reason, to be much more barren of architectural development than the previous time of building activity had been.

It was not until the early 1940's that building started again in any volume. Even then, no great strides in either the esthetics or the technology of architecture were immediately visible, although much of interest was going on below the surface, as we shall see. And to extend the apparent hiatus in design growth, the Second World War made impossible the building of any but essential civil and military structures for its duration. In fact, the history of United States architecture, so far as it can be demonstrated by important completed buildings, picks up again only at the end of the war in 1946.

It is necessary, nevertheless, to examine the ideas, the personalities and the research activities that were gestating and growing through these periods of boom, depression, and war. Afterward, when building started again, there was a realization that certain basically important things had been learned during the hectic, eclectic activity of the 1920's. In retrospect, it could even be considered that the comparative inactivity during the depression that followed had had its healthy aspects. There had been time to think, to re-evaluate, to experiment, to look more closely at what had been happening in other parts of the world, and to make plans for the time when architects would again have clients eager and able to build. During the war years, when many basic materials were scarce, a new respect for simplicity and directness in building developed, along with a necessarily experimental attitude.

What were the advances that had been made between 1920 and 1946?

First of all, a series of important technical developments had taken place. Great strides had been made in the use of a metal frame since the earlier days of the Chicago experiments. The large steel companies had reached a point of production that allowed standard structural sections, and the construction industry had found ways to erect these columns and beams to a great height. Mechanical equipment, electrically operated, now made possible a high degree of control over the interior environment, and ventilating and even air conditioning had become standard for many types of buildings. The lighting of interior spaces had become a much more sophisticated art than at any previous time.

In addition to steel, other structural materials, even such a traditional one as wood, were finding new applications with the lamination of timbers (the gluing together of a number of pieces in layers), the bending of wood members to form arches, and rigid structural connectors. Newer building products that did not yet boast the ability to bear heavy loads but were nonetheless important, were forming the bases of new, great industries: aluminum in various alloys, plastics, glass of unexpected qualities. The industrial revolution, in short, had its effect on architecture, but the architects were slow—as they have been in all periods of history—to consider what effect new technologies might have on the design of their buildings.

There was also much to be learned and evaluated from developments that had taken place during this time in Western Europe. While the influence of the *Beaux Arts* school continued strong in the U.S., and the work of Frank Lloyd Wright and the few native "modernists" was largely ignored, the strength of the *Beaux Arts* method of teaching and practicing architecture was being challenged in Europe by new philosophies and schools of design. There the arguments of Wright for an "organic" architecture, growing as does a natural organism from its particular location and situation and from natural materials, and the illustrations of his ideas in the few but important buildings he had been able to complete, were increasingly influential.

In Europe in the teens and the twenties, in fact, there was in preparation the next wave of architectural influence that was to sweep the slate of United States architecture clean of its remaining pseudo-traditional design. There was the early work of Walter Gropius, the German architect who headed the famous *Bauhaus* school, where architecture and the other arts were fused in an attempt to express the use of machine-made products. Marking an almost clean break with the other work of the time, the buildings that Gropius and his colleagues designed were virtually unknown for a long while in the United States.

There were many other groups. There was the work of the Futurists, denying Gropius's functionalist approach and in many ways reminiscent of Wright's organic attitude. There was the simplicity, directness and functionalism of Ludwig Mies van de Rohe in Germany, strongly expressed in several early buildings that have become classics of the modern movement. There was the movement known as *De Stijl*, beginning in Holland, closely relating new styles in architecture, painting, and sculpture that were similar in their use of flat planes and straight, connecting lines. There was the development of a strong creative talent in France, the Swiss-born architect Le Corbusier. Building on the experiments in concrete design of the French architect-engineers Tony Garnier and Auguste Perret, and on the Cubist studies in painting and sculpture, he developed an architectural form of his own that has matured continually since the 1920's. And influencing the thinking and the design experiments of almost all of these innovators was the work of Wright in the United States, published first in Europe in 1910 and 1911.

Although contemporary experiments often seemed to be in conflict and the innovators sometimes were bitterly jealous of one another, they constituted in total a radical departure from the way buildings were being designed and were being built conventionally in the United States.

It has been remarked before that America has often absorbed and adapted architectural influences from abroad. Perhaps the most significant instance of this continuing phenomenon is the way the early modern stirrings in Europe have been transplanted to the United States, carried to the point of active accomplishment through American technological skill, and then again made available to other countries. The curiosity and the perspicacity of two American scholar-architects—Philip C. Johnson and Henry-Russell Hitchcock—brought the work of many of the seemingly diverse modern European schools into one exhibition in New York, in 1932, at the Museum of Modern Art. This show and a book they wrote at the same time tagged the new movement "The International Style" and dated the beginning of the next phase in architecture in America.

As it did develop in America, this period of modernism in architecture was characterized primarily by its esthetics: a series of flat planes, perhaps of masonry, perhaps of concrete or even stucco, perhaps of sheets of glass, that intersected and defined interior spaces without the conscious building of a wall that separated one area from another, and without the puncturing of that wall with arbitrarily designed doors and windows. It was an architecture of flowing space and freedom in the interruption or the direction of that space, by the positioning of plane surfaces. Technologically, it paid lip service to the use of factory-made products and machine-produced finishes; in actuality, its buildings were erected by quite traditional methods, and the materials used were for the most part still hand-fabricated, hand-poured, or hand-assembled. It expressed the contemporary world, even if it did not fully exploit contemporary technologies.

The development of this period of modernism in architecture was hastened by the movement of many of the European modernists to American shores. Some had, indeed, come earlier. By 1929, Richard J. Neutra, a Viennese, was already designing open, richly glazed, simply constructed houses in California: houses that seemed remarkably adapted to the terrain and the climate. William Lescaze, a Swiss, had associated with George Howe, a Philadelphia architect of conservative background, to build the Philadelphia Savings Fund Society building in that

Philadelphia Savings Fund Society, Philadelphia, Pennsylvania
Architect: GEORGE HOWE & WILLIAM LESCAZE

city. It was one of the first of the fully modern skyscrapers that from now on began to deny Sullivan's dictum that even a non-traditional high building must have a base, a shaft, and a *cap*. R. M. Schindler and Raphael S. Soriano in California; Erich Mendelsohn, one of the strong European expressionists, who also moved to the West Coast; Frederick Kiesler, a neo-plasticist and a member of the de Stijl group, who has been markedly influential despite few constructed works; Antonin Raymond, Oskar Stonorov—these and many others were already here when the better-known leaders came, shortly before the beginnings of the Second World War. Walter Gropius was called to Harvard in 1937, and he brought with him his most talented architectural student from the Bauhaus, Marcel Breuer. Lazlo Moholy-Nagy founded the New Bauhaus in Chicago. Mies van der Rohe was called to Illinois Institute of Technology at about the same time.

Undoubtedly one reason that the influence of these men became so great so quickly in the United States is that they were brought to America to teach. In time they all also established practices, but that is part of the story of the post-war period. The important thing to recall, in this review of the developments during the 1920's and 1930's, is that they began immediately to influence students in American schools of architecture. By the end of World War II, the entire method of teaching design had changed, in all but some of the smaller schools in the more conservative states. By that time some of the students of Gropius and Mies van der Rohe were ready to begin practice and to bring to bear an attitude totally different in every respect from that of their elders.

One further important note must be made before we leave the discussion of changing design philosophies to look at other growing influences. That is the fact that there was a maturing group of younger native architects who had begun to express themselves in very belligerent fashion before the war—even before the influx from abroad assumed its full proportions. Gregory Ain, Pietro Belluschi, George Fred Kock, Ernest J. Kump, G. Holmes Perkins, Ralph Rapson, A. G. Jan Ruhtenberg, Edward D. Stone, Hugh A. Stubbins and others revolted against the older generation's unwillingness to experiment and were finding clients who would sponsor contemporary houses and even occasionally churches and schools. Frank Lloyd Wright had founded, at his two home-school headquarters that he called Taliesin (one built early in Wisconsin, the other constructed during the 1920's in Arizona) a fellowship teaching method. The Taliesin Fellowship produced many non-traditionalists, most of whom were so completely indoctrinated Wrightists, however, that they lacked strong expressive qualities of their own. At Cranbrook Academy in Detroit, Michigan, the elder Saarinen, Eliel, taught architecture. He came to the United States in the early 1920's from Finland, where he left a brilliant practice after nearly winning an international competition for the design of a home for a Chicago newspaper—the Chicago Tribune Tower. His school spawned many extremely talented designers, who seemed neither traditionalist nor too fully indoctrinated in the romantic modern approach of Saarinen himself.

During this same time in California, both around the San Francisco Bay region, where William Wilson Wurster and Gardner A. Dailey—two local architects with a great concern for native influences—showed the way, and in the Los Angeles area, where Neutra, Schindler, and Soriano were leaders, there developed a regional architecture that respected Maybeck and earlier California architects, and yet was in no sense traditional or eclectic.

5

ARCHITECTURE AND SOCIAL PLANNING

Before we discuss the next phase of architecture in the United States, we must realize other changes in attitude that had taken place between the stock market crash of 1929 and the end of the war in 1946. Even before the onset of the depression, there had been concern on the part of many planners, sociologists, economists—and some architects—about the social aspects of building. There was in the boom years of the 1920's a somewhat heedless rush to build for commerce and industry and for the wealthier groups who controlled and profited from these activities. Meanwhile the growing physical needs of the more numerous lower-incomed parts of the population were often ignored. Beyond that, there was concern that the environment itself might be irretrievably despoiled by the unplanned growth of cities and the suburbs that were encircling them. And still further, there were farsighted planners in and out of government who saw the need to develop natural and social resources sensibly. A nation's resources, they pointed out, are not only physical assets such as timber and water-power sources, but include such human assets as the health, the educational development, and even the cultural growth of the community.

The activities of the New Deal, during the administrations of President Franklin Delano Roosevelt, did much to forward the study of subjects of this kind. There was a new, socially-oriented philosophy of government; there was the need to provide work by public building; and there were many thinkers and doers ready to take advantage of the situation. Thus there arose, as important subjects for study, the problems of physical planning on a greater scale than most architects had been concerned with before; housing for lower income groups; the development of ideal communities; the setting up of a national program of hospital and health facilities; study of the adequacy of the educational plant; concern with the nature and effect of the rapidly expanding urban environment. These became topics for conferences, new organizations, written literature, research under government and university auspices.

A corps of dedicated and hard-working people formed an almost new profession of "housers and planners" in the late 1920's and the 1930's: Lewis Mumford, who is still today a respected critic and theorist; Catherine Bauer, teacher, writer, and theorist (who later married the architect William Wilson Wurster); Henry Wright, Sr. and Clarence S. Stein, architect-planners, who had built or inspired the building of several green-belted towns with some concern for privacy and with limitations of growth. Places like Radburn, New Jersey (of which, unhappily, there are not many) showed how a community could be self-centered, yet related to surrounding developments, and could be so planned as to separate living spaces from automobile traffic and allow a sense of landscaped privacy.

Other groups were also articulate on the subject of social planning, but were more concerned with the architecture of dams and other "modern monuments" and with the development of recreation areas and national parks and reserves. Still others were most interested in formulating a planned national network of related health facilities, from the small clinic to the great metropolitan medical center; or in a similar study of the educational facility from kindergartens to graduate universities.

Marshall Shaffer, an architect who had worked with Neutra in California and later devoted his life to administering the federal government's Hill-Burton Hospital construction program (a means of providing funds to local communities for hospital construction); Vernon DeMars, concerned with housing problems; and others in such diverse fields as school design or prefabrication of houses could be cited as instances of a new brand of architect, a kind of social-designer-planner who made his own contribution to the mixture of background factors that lay ready to produce the architecture of the 1940's, the post-war years that lead directly to the present condition of U.S. architecture.

6

THE POST-WAR RESURGENCE

As the Second World War drew to a close, it became apparent that there would be a great surge of new building activity. It was not so clear, however, what direction the design of the new buildings would take. For a long time the wartime restrictions on construction had halted even the most necessary activity; there was a backlog of real need in housing, in schools and hospitals and in all sorts of community and government buildings. In the meantime, the population curve had prepared itself for a sharp upward movement, so that it was possible to foresee an even greater need for shelter houses and apartments. But it was very difficult to know which of the many influences now reaching architects in the United States would be most influential. A book written at the end of the war, attempting such a forecast, dealt largely with the technological advance that was inevitable, in heating and cooling methods, in the use of new and newly improved materials, and in the fuller understanding of the structural behavior of building forms. Further than that, it pointed to the freedom that existed in design, now that the hold of traditional eclecticism was broken in so many places, and to the freedom that the new architect had in solving problems realistically and functionally.

At first the freedom had to be proven. On the surface it appeared that "the battle for modern architecture has been won," as the Museum of Modern Art expressed it. By the end of the war, all of the national architectural magazines were giving more and more space to articles about "modern" architecture, and were actively editorializing for its acceptance. The few holdouts among the schools of architecture also began teaching contemporary design, urging many of their graduates to remain as teachers. And more and more clients began accepting the newer designs. Yet there was no clear definition of "modern," and older architects, with a background of practice in traditional styles, fought hard and sometimes viciously against the trend. It was in this situation that the architects in the United States began to absorb the lessons learned from abroad. Slowly they assimilated the Europeans who had come here to teach and practice, then found ways to add their own technological innovations and applied all of these factors to needs and potentials in the United States. In short, they set out to produce an American architecture that became, in the 1950's and early 1960's, the dominant influence throughout the world.

Even in the early years of the triumph of modernism over traditionalism, there was never a clear, single design trend. There were those (Paul Schweikher, Alden B. Dow, Karl Kamrath, Bruce Goff, and others) who followed Frank Lloyd Wright's desire for an architecture that grew from the soil, but both in Wright's own work and in that of the architects influenced by him, there too soon appeared a kind of romantic fantasy.

There were those, a greater number of them, who saw merit in the more down-to-earth, functionally-oriented, technologically-inclined direction indicated by Walter Gropius and especially Mies van der Rohe. The reasons for this were many, but perhaps the most important one was that Mies's concern with simple expression of the materials of construction—primarily a steel frame, with large glass areas within the frame—was immediately applicable to the continuing American interest in a metal-framed structure. It was consistent with the developing manufacture of factory-made, repetitive building parts, and it lent itself to rapid processes of erection and completion of buildings. Furthermore, while Wright demonstrated a style of *design* to his students, Gropius and Mies were more inclined to teach *principles* ("less is more," said Mies), and their students soon became leaders among the younger group of architects, often departing strongly from the exact design manner of their masters. What they had learned was a discipline, a refinement of simple elements, a sense of proportion, and a respect for contemporary technology. All of these principles seemed to fit well into the growing practices of large firms such as Skidmore, Owings & Merrill, Harrison & Abramovitz, and others. Thus within a short time a somewhat commercialized version of what, in the 1930's, had been called the International Style, became the popular skyscraper design, accepted alike by those who commissioned the buildings and those who financed them. In the hands of an extremely sensitive designer of large buildings such as Gordon Bunshaft (the principal design partner of Skidmore, Owings & Merrill) or perfectionists in small building design such as Craig Elwood or Raphael Soriano, these same principles could develop into an American esthetic—a philosophy of design as well as a functional and economic solution. How this approach to tall building design reached a point of glass-walled monotony is another story to be told later.

At the same time that Wright had his late followers and his own growing practice, and Mies and Gropius were proving themselves such successful teachers, the regional expression on the West Coast that had followed from Maybeck and the Greene Brothers also had its post-war heyday. For some years after the war the residential work, particularly of people such as Henry Hill, John Dinwiddie, John Funk, Harwell Harris, and, in the northwest, John Yeon, Paul Hayden Kirk, and others was the most frequently published style in the professional architectural magazines, and then later in the popular home journals.

In 1950, in fact, one of the architectural magazines, reviewing the half century and taking stock at mid-point, saw three contributing, if not conflicting, approaches to design: the naturally growing, organic design of Wright, the technical logic of Mies, and the regional humanism—based primarily on the use of local woods—of what had come to be called the Bay Area Style, centering around San Francisco, California.

But post-war architecture did not remain divided into simple categories. Another strong tendency, as the architect gained freedom to design to the particular program of his client, was toward individualism and "appropriate" expressions, almost all different from one another and departing from any antecedents, even recent ones. There were many reasons why this should happen. The classic disciplines had been discarded. In order to design "correctly" it was no longer necessary to follow the dictates of Vitruvius, the first century B.C. Roman architect whose rules of proportion have guided architects through most of the periods since his time. In place of classic rules there had been substituted for a time the dogmas of the International Style, just as doctrinaire and as rigid: buildings should be simple, direct, expressive of structure and of function, with no extraneous frivolities or decorations added. Many of the younger architects soon found these ideologies too restrictive and rebelled against them.

In addition, disciplines based on regionalism were rapidly disappearing. As communication facilities and travel opportunities increased, as populations shifted to and from various parts of the country, regional differences were minimized. As materials once indigenous to a certain area became equally available in others, and as attitudes, styles of living, and educational backgrounds became more and more similar across the country, regional architectural stylisms seemed less valid. They came to seem forced, arbitrary, and superficial.

40

Another important reason for the appearance of variation in design was a loosening of the grip of the steel frame, with which the earlier modern movement was largely identified. Architects began to study the plastic possibilities of concrete and the opportunities it opened up for individual expression.

For these reasons and others, as the decade of the 1950's drew to a close, a great variety in design in America began to appear, perhaps most importantly in the work of those architects most admired by their colleagues. Paul Rudolph, raised to fame as a designer when he was a young man with very few buildings to his credit (a Gropius graduate from Harvard) developed an interest in plasticity—irregular broken forms adapting themselves to what he saw as the functional needs of a building—which denied both traditional classicism and traditional modernism. His architectural school building at Yale University, in New Haven, Connecticut, is an interesting instance. Eero Saarinen, firmly established in his own practice

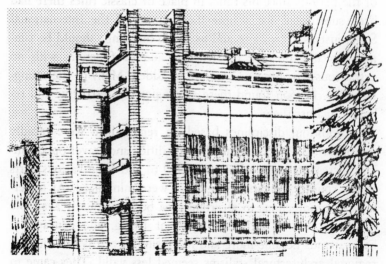

School of Architecture, Yale University, New Haven, Connecticut
Architect: PAUL RUDOLPH

after his father Eliel's death, demonstrated his gifts by designing a round form as a chapel and a domed form as an auditorium, both at M.I.T. In addition he conceived a winged form as an air terminal at the Kennedy International Airport in New York, a teepee form as a college building in Indiana, and a glass-walled rectangular form as a research center for the General Motors Corporation in Detroit, Michigan. Then, shortly before his own death in 1961, he designed a completely original slung roof hanging from great sculptured piers as another air terminal form, at Dulles International Airport in Washington, D.C. Even Gordon Bunshaft and Walter A. Netsch, Jr., the two senior design partners of Skidmore, Owings & Merrill, began to be restive within the Miesian discipline they had adapted so handsomely. They toyed with concrete, as in the Rare Book Library at Yale by Bunshaft, or with very plastic geometries in metal as in Netsch's chapel at the Air Force Academy in Colorado.

In the early 1960's, the magazine *Progressive Architecture* attempted to assess the state of design by conducting a symposium among the leading practitioners. When they were asked whether there was not an almost confusing diversity of design approach, they admitted—and justified—the situation. They pointed out that American society past the mid-century mark was not restricted to one philosophy, one political attitude, nor even one religion. It embraced differing points of view in a democratic manner. Many types of buildings for many purposes to be used by many kinds of people, in this sort of society, demand many design solutions, the architects contended. And in addition, they argued, the variety of materials available and the endless structural schemes possible with today's engineering skills, are not likely to produce an architecture of a single style.

Thus there are today a great many approaches to architecture in the United States. One sees thin-shell concrete structures, domed and curved in many ways, poured with great accuracy. One still sees metal and glass "curtain" walls on tall buildings. There is even a returning interest in history, and without exact eclectic copying, some of the best designers have looked to the past once more. Paul Rudolph has been able to recall Gothic detail in his Jewett Arts Center at Wellesley College, and Philip Johnson has rediscovered classic intersecting vaults in one of his buildings. Saarinen was happy to design two new colleges at Yale with obvious medieval leanings, complete with contemporary sculpture that recalled gargoyles. Skidmore, Owings & Merrill used arches on the lower floor of a San Francisco skyscraper, the John Hancock Building, that recalled earlier work in that city.

Newly found structural forms such as the hyperbolic paraboloid (a series of intersecting curved surfaces built up or "generated" from straight lines) and the folded plate roof (a sawtooth design like that produced by folding paper in successive bends) became, in a short while, so common that architects tended to turn quickly from them to find something even newer and, hopefully, more original. The Vierendeel truss, a simple box-like structure that makes great spans possible in certain types of buildings, threatened in its turn to become the next cliché. A number of the architects who had tired of rigid disciplines and unornamented surfaces reached for "delight" in architecture, as Minoru Yamasaki expressed it, or a richness, as Edward Durell Stone said, that led them to tracery-like *mullions* between windows, vaulted roof forms instead of flat roofs, and even applied ornament. Although some of this more sensual design ran the risk of being superficial, often lacking the bold originality that Louis Sullivan had achieved, it did add more variety and humanism to the architectural scene.

In very recent years, there has been another of the many instances in our history of an influence from abroad, studied and made use of in such a way that it becomes in time truly American. The new influence is the almost brutal plasticity, expressed characteristically in concrete, that marks the work of Le Corbusier. His work is brutal because forms and finishes are purposely rugged; it is plastic because surfaces seem pushed and pulled to suit the concept. After periods in his work of very arbitrary and formal design and then of a direct simplicity related to the International Style, the Swiss-French architect turned in his own post-war development to an extremely plastic irregularity in the face of the building, bringing out parts that he wanted to emphasize, recessing others for an equal emphasis, raising his structures on sculptured posts (which he called *pilotis,* stilts), giving the basic forms themselves any character that he thought appropriate, using window and door openings as a painter would use lines and areas to build a composition.

His favorite material, concrete, gives him the sculptural freedom that he wants, and his favorite way of using it, with rough forms, produces the brutally rugged effect. With all this freedom, he disciplines himself through a complicated system of proportioning of his own devising, based on human anatomy, that he has named the Modulor. He sees architecture as would a painter or a sculptor—both of which, indeed, he is. Two well-known buildings of his in France—an apartment house in Marseilles and a church at Ronchamp—have been particularly influential in the United States.

It would almost seem that the individual work of Le Corbusier, though tremendously admired by American architects, could be as little translated into a "trend" that others might follow as could Wright's work. And yet around him has grown a cult of admirers: New Brutalists, as some of them have been called (indicating their love of rugged, almost crude forms); Plasticists, as others like to be known (expressing their wish to warp and pull a form to fit its particular purpose); experimenters in expressive concrete form as many of them basically are. In the United States Louis I. Kahn, a Philadelphia architect who late in his life has had both success in practice and renown as a teacher, is the most articulate one among those affected by Le Corbusier's approach. In his own office and at the University of Pennsylvania where he teaches, he has influenced many younger people directly. The indirect effect of his work has been very great on those who have simply seen one of his buildings (the Richards Medical Research Building at the University of Pennsylvania, at once his most admired and most controversial work) or merely studied his published designs.

Alfred Newton Richards Medical Research Building,
University of Pennsylvania, Philadelphia, Pennsylvania
Architect: Louis Kahn

It would seem to be a reasonable guess that this influence will increase, and that "action architecture," as one of the younger architects has called it (relating it to abstract-expressionist painting) will be, for a time at least, the next dominant phase of U.S. architecture. An instance of the spreading acceptance of this new "style" in the 1960's was the winning of a competition for design of a new City Hall in Boston, Massachusetts by three designers—Kallman, McKinnell and Knowles—in the "brutal" plastic manner. Kahn's influence may not be long-lived, because one can tire quickly of a rather naïve philosophy of esthetics that he expresses with endless conviction. However, the deeper impact of Le Corbusier, as the great form maker, seems to have possibilities of outlasting that of Wright, as the great moulder of organic space, or Mies, as the great disciplined technician, in the continuing history of architecture in the United States.

The status of that architecture at the present time in history, and the extent of its contribution to architectural development in other parts of the world, must be evaluated in relation to the advances that have been made in design of specific building types and in changing methods of practice. That is what the next chapters in this book will attempt to do. However, before we conclude the rapid chronological survey that has been made up to this point, certain positive conclusions can be drawn.

Architecture in the United States (aside from that of the earlier Indian civilizations) is less than three centuries old. That it could, in that time and under the conditions of its development, produce the number of creative designers, the multitude of interesting and often historically important buildings, and the many technological innovations that it has, is remarkable. It has never evolved a "style," and that is probably a very good thing. A part of the contribution that the United States of America can make to an expanding, a developing, and a maturing world is its bold willingness to continue trying new ideas, as well as its ability to discipline these youthful characteristics sufficiently to produce usable objects. Those are the qualities of its architecture—rather than the success or failure of individual efforts, important and interesting as they may be —that make the United States a leader today in esthetic and technological experiment.

PART II
THE ARCHITECTURAL SCENE TODAY

1.

VIRTUES AND FAULTS

If it is possible to learn about a society by the architecture it produces, what conclusions can one draw about the United States in the 1960's from looking at the buildings that exist and those that are being constructed in such great numbers day by day?

At first glance the view is a confused one. The face that most cities present to the traveler, or even to their own citizens, is often composed of a medley of styles that mark the periods of taste when they were used, and a mixture of materials that may denote economy or affluence or again simply the fashion of the moment. There is a common gridiron plan along the streets and avenues on which the buildings are strung, often with little relation to one another; a profusion of signs and lights and poles and wires that further confuse the view. And everywhere there are automobiles, parked in every open space, moving along each line of the grid. This is the view of America beyond which many critics, foreign and native, have failed to see.

But for one who looks deeper, the view is not that bad. In fact, the advances that have been made in almost every aspect of architecture are so great that architects and architectural students come from many countries to the United States, to study and to learn from what has been done here. In the planning of many building types, in the technology of construction, in efforts to improve the urban environment, no nation today can point to more research, study, or actual achievements.

How can one reconcile these different views of the scene? In the first place, even the sometimes unsightly surface itself is not as faulty as it seems. Most of the American cityscape is raw and new, as has been remarked; in the history of American architecture one speaks of time only a century ago as if it were far in the past. Colonial Williamsburg in Virginia is reconstructed and revered, as it should be, but compared to the preserved monuments of the older civilizations and the earlier-formed countries of Europe, it is almost current history. In a few centuries the United States has built a great nation and has had to build also the houses and churches and schools and public buildings that that nation needed. They have been erected quickly, and in many cases they have been torn down and replaced just as rapidly.

There is something brightly naïve along with the crudities, something fresh even in the deterioration, something brave and vigorous along with the brashness and thoughtlessness, in the typical American city. And in the great metropolitan centers there is character of a sort that few older cities have: San Francisco, with its frankly ugly, bay-windowed houses ranging up and down the unplanned hills; New York with its magnificent skyline formed by individually undistinguished buildings and its crowded heartless heart; Chicago, with its great waterfront lying next to a gloomy loop of noisy traffic. The surface of the American city may be a visual hodgepodge, but it has character—a character of vigor and activity and accomplishment.

When one goes out beyond the teeming centers of the cities, into the suburbs and the subdivisions that connect one urban center to the next, and even into the remaining rural areas and the small towns that are becoming ever less isolated, there is a double picture also. The speculative nature of much single-family housing and the lack of high quality in both design and construction of much home building have been rightly deplored by social as well as architectural critics. On the other hand, the volume of this building, the speed of its erection, the conveniences that are built into the houses, the number of people of various economic levels who are accommodated in them—these characteristics again have been remarked and admired by entrepreneurs from other lands, who are often not able to do as well in today's economy.

The faults in American architecture, then, are obvious ones: there is insufficient planning of where buildings should go and how the total physical landscape should grow (which is a way of saying that building is too rapid); there is insufficient attention paid to design (which is a way of saying that the popular level of esthetic taste is not as high as it should be). Speed, and naïveté in taste, however, are not incurable faults. Speed can be controlled and checked, and this is being done more and more through planning agencies, redevelopment authorities, and zoning and building codes. Design understanding can be improved through education and greater maturity, and this is happening to a constantly increasing degree. The faults are unfortunately obvious: the great good points about architecture in the United States today must be studied to be seen.

The characteristic of the American people called "know-how"—the determination to learn how to do a thing better than it had been done before—appears most clear when one studies the new buildings type by type. In general, buildings fall into a few major functional categories: housing, education, health, commerce, industry, religion, public use. In a complicated modern society the sub-categories under these headings become ever more numerous; for instance, group medical practice has brought new requirements in building for health-care purposes; the junior college is a recently important factor in the educational field. But the categories mentioned continue to provide the principal impetus to new construction.

2.

BUILDINGS FOR COMMERCE

Of all the commercial structures that have been developed in the United States, the tall office building—the skyscraper—is at once the most dramatic and the most significant. Since the earliest probes skyward before 1900, principally in New York and Chicago, this piling of office floors one on another has continued to as great a height as construction materials and vertical transportation devices would allow. The economic reasons, principally the use of high-priced urban land to its maximum capacity, are compelling; the esthetic and technical problems raised are fascinating; but the human and social effects have only recently been fully understood.

Obviously, extremely tall buildings must be as light as possible in construction, else the problem of foundations becomes too great. (In some of the earlier skyscrapers, substructures were almost as deep as the superstructures were tall.) The step from masonry walls that carried the weight of the floors above to a steel frame was a major one; the next great advance in skill was the development of an infill between the steel columns that could be truly a curtain, designed only to keep out inclement weather, and not as an unneeded wall.

The "curtain wall," consisting of an insulated metal and glass skin hung from the structural frame, has in recent years become a common sight in American cities, and has been one of the features of U.S. architecture copied throughout the world, even where it often seems inappropriate. The esthetic problem of designing a thin, flat, grid-patterned wall is a diffi-

Lever House, New York City, New York
Architect: SKIDMORE, OWINGS & MERRILL

51

cult one. The difference between banality and monotony, on the one hand, and elegance and richness on the other, lies only in the delicacy of dimensions of the metal mullions that separate the glass panels and the refinement of proportion of the window openings and the vertical and horizontal separations between them.

In the hands of architect-artists, some of these buildings are indeed beautiful. Skidmore, Owings & Merrill, the firm that has done most with the problem, can boast one of the earliest successes in Lever House in New York; one of the best of the Midwest examples, in the Inland Steel Building in Chicago; one of the few sensitive instances on the West Coast, in the Crown Zellerbach Building in San Francisco; and one of the largest and most impressive, in the Chase Manhattan Bank building in downtown New York. Undoubtedly the gem of them all is the Seagram House, on Park Avenue in New York, designed by Mies van der Rohe and Philip Johnson who used bronze as the curtain material. In Pittsburgh, Harrison & Abramovitz used stainless steel in one building and, in another, experimented with an aluminum curtain wall, where windows were small and the aluminum spandrels (the panels between openings) were bent and patterned to give them stiffness. Wallace K. Harrison, partner in this New York firm, did the local coordination and production work on the United Nations headquarters—one of the early curtain-wall buildings in New York, conceived originally by an international group of architects.

Not all the tall buildings were as successful. Firms such as Emery Roth & Sons in New York found that is was possible to develop formulas for maximum production of rentable space on a given plot of land, and were able to adapt the curtain-wall construction system to almost any form configuration—deep, shallow, tall, short, even stepped back in multiple layers. The Roth firm—now headed by two sons and a grandson of the

53

founder—has designed scores of post-war apartment houses as well as office buildings in New York. They have proved (by trying everything else) that the single sheer tower, such as Seagram's, is the most exciting esthetic solution to the skyscraper, if not always the one most productive of revenue.

In recent years, a renewed interest in concrete has led to studies of the potential of this material as a frame for highrise buildings (some structures up to thirty stories have been built), or simply as a curtain material used in the form of precast panels raised into place. I. M. Pei (a Chinese-born Gropius-trained architect who has risen rapidly to the top echelon of U.S. designers), Skidmore, Owings & Merrill, and

United Nations Headquarters, New York City, New York
Architect: WALLACE K. HARRISON et. al.

the Roth firm, among others, have experimented in this direction. In still further developments, the use of precast, prestressed concrete elements that would serve both as bearing frame (columns, beams, girders) and as infill wall has been tried. Precasting is the manufacture of large elements away from the building site, under controlled conditions. Prestressing is a method of stretching the steel reinforcing rods taut, so that there will be less bending when the precast part is installed. Steel also is showing new qualities, and in a building for the Equitable Life Insurance Company in Pittsburgh, Pennsylvania, architects Curtis & Davis (a New Orleans firm doing distinguished work now in many parts of the world) are using new high-strength steels in a diagonal grid pattern which forms the entire façade, with windows in the diamonds.

Fairly early in the development of the skyscraper, it was realized that the tall buildings introduced problems of congestion in the neighborhoods in which they were built—crowded transportation facilities for the thousands of people working in the buildings and clogged restaurants and stores around the buildings. They also brought problems of light and air in the streets along which they rose. Limitations of height have been set, by various formulas, in most large cities: some communities have devised ways to encourage less than full coverage of a plot of land so that small islands of space might be left along the avenues; some require parking facilities within the buildings so that the streets are less blocked by cars (a questionable result, since the parking privileges bring more cars to the building).

Some critics have called those tall commercial buildings sterile and the streets they line monotonous walls of glass. The other view is that the reflections in the continuing glass face, the repetition of nearly similar modules, the very lack of shades and shadows and of differentiation of planes brings an esthetic result that is clean and fresh and modern and handsome in its own way. The most valid criticism is that scale is often lacking; the relation of the sheer wall to human size is hard to establish. Primarily for this reason many architects have tried, in design, to break the flat façade. I. M. Pei has suggested schemes with great corner piers connected by equally bold trusses that span the building at floor level. Anshen & Allen (San Francisco design-conscious partners) won the top award for excellence in design of the American Institute of Architects in 1963 with their International Building in San Francisco. This is an office building with the horizontality of each floor emphasized, rather than the verticality of the entire building. The corners are *notched off,* to provide room for ventilation ducts to run up the building in these locations. The result is handsome, recalling, at larger scale but perhaps with less subtlety, Frank Lloyd Wright's one completed tall building— the Price Tower in Bartlesville, Oklahoma. Paul Rudolph, in his Blue Cross Building in Boston, also used vertical mechanical duct systems, expressed in regular piers along the sides of the building, to provide an exterior design element.

The interiors of these great office buildings have received their share of technological attention also. Air conditioning has made possible use of much deeper interior space than when perimeter ventilation from the windows was needed for all offices; and the development of ceiling lighting systems and movable, flexible partitioning systems (often integrated into one related ceiling-and-partition system) have made this interior space more comfortable.

To move the discussion to other sorts of commercial buildings, a fairly new architectural problem—at least new in its contemporary application—is the "shopping center" that may serve a fairly large region. The department store is not a new idea in merchandising in the United States, nor in many other countries. But the idea of grouping together in one complex many small stores that might gather around a central department store, and providing numerous facilities for those who come to buy many things, is a recent one. The more ambitious shopping centers even furnish some recreational opportunities, including classes in sculpture and painting, perhaps a concert hall or a community meeting space.

These groups of community or regional stores require careful planning and an acute knowledge of both merchandising techniques and population trends, before esthetics can even be thought of. Nevertheless, some architects such as Victor Gruen, having applied design skills to this problem, have produced, as at J. L. Hudson's Northland and Eastland Centers in Detroit, a cohesive and a handsome result. Gruen and his partners, with

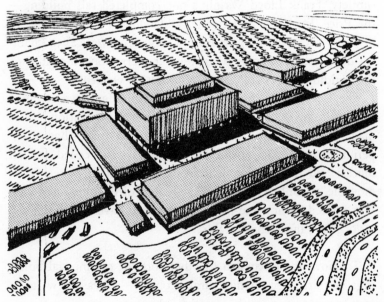

Eastland Shopping Center, Detroit, Michigan
Architect: VICTOR GRUEN

headquarters in Los Angeles, have realized that an architect's responsibilities now extend beyond esthetics, and they have made great contributions to such broader planning subjects as the regional shopping center.

Among the many other modern commercial activities that require shelter, transportation has had a great effect on architectural developments in the United States. In addition to parking garages, some of which have been of striking design, and great bus terminals, few of which have been distinguished, the growing number of terminal buildings for air travel has brought many interesting solutions. The problem is common throughout the world, of course, but nowhere else have the answers been so large in scale, or so bold. Kennedy International Airport in New York is composed largely of a series of individual—and individually designed—terminals surrounding a great central parking area. The disparateness which results from having no central design control and no theme is visually confusing, and circulation from one airline to another is not easy. Some of the buildings, however—particularly Eero Saarinen's TWA Terminal, in concrete wing-like forms that suggest flight—are extremely interesting. The terminal building at St. Louis, Missouri, designed by the firm of Hellmuth, Yamasaki and Leinweber is outstanding with great open spaces formed by three domed forms that meet and join. O'Hare Field's terminal in Chicago, of which the Chicago architect Albert Shaw is designer, is a handsome, simple, rectangular solution.

In structures such as these, various solutions to the problem of separating incoming and outgoing passengers, and eliminating confusion between baggage transfer and passenger circulation, have been tried. But the difficulty in getting large numbers of people from the building to the plane itself, usually solved by long passages extending from the waiting rooms to the plane stations, has been most boldly attacked in Saarinen's terminal at Dulles International Airport near Washington, D.C. There he used "mobile lounges"—comfortably furnished autobuses that detach themselves from the terminal building, transport passengers to the aircraft, and so allow them to walk directly to their seats.

Dulles International Airport, Washington, D.C.
Architect: EERO SAARINEN

3.

BUILDINGS FOR RELIGIOUS USE

Churches and temples in the United States have gone through many phases since the New England meeting house, as we have seen, marked a new approach to this type of build-

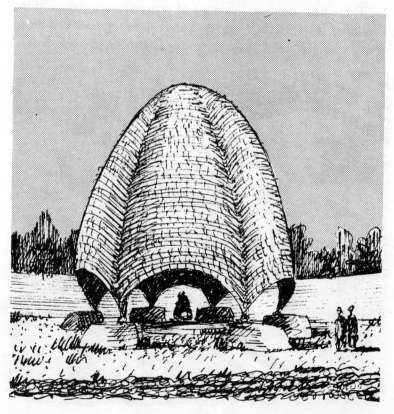

New Harmony Shrine, New Harmony, Indiana
Architect: PHILLIP C. JOHNSON

ing. The efforts to find new, appropriate ways of housing usually ages-old ritualistic ceremonies have been many. Pietro Belluschi, an Italian-born architect who practiced in Portland, Oregon, until he became Dean of the M. I. T. School of Architecture and Planning, designed beautifully dignified contemporary brick and wood church buildings in the Northwest. In a way, those warm and appealing buildings were similar to several soft-lighted, simple wood and brick churches by the elder Saarinen which, for a time, set an almost romantic style.

There have been various ways of expressing aspiration in the building form itself. Victor A. Lundy, a young, talented architect, who has used inwardly curved, laminated roof beams,

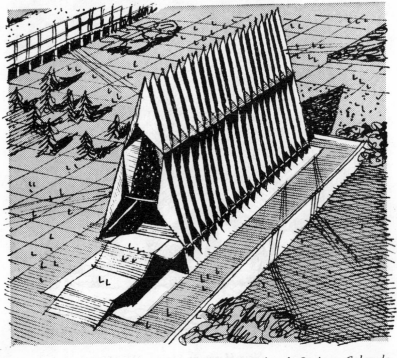

Air Force Academy Chapel, Colorado Springs, Colorado
Architect: SKIDMORE, OWINGS & MERRILL

almost recalling inverted ship hulls, sometimes separated at the top to allow light to filter through, has successful achievements to his credit in Florida and in Connecticut. Mies van der Rohe and his followers used their rectangular, exposed steel grids even for religious buildings—for instance, in his chapel at the Illinois Institute of Technology. Sculptural forms have been tried, as in Philip Johnson's New Harmony Shrine in Indiana where a huge, softly curved roof is covered with shingles. And geometric forms have also been used, as in Skidmore, Owings & Merrill's Chapel for Three Faiths designed by Walter Netsch at the Air Force Academy in Colorado, where the geometric figure known as a tetrahedron has been compressed, stood on end, and repeated almost as a series of spires.

4.

BUILDINGS FOR INDUSTRY

The giant companies of industry and commerce in the United States have often built themselves fine architectural headquarters for office use in recent years. The Hartford Life Insurance Company headquarters in Connecticut, designed by the ubiquitous firm of Skidmore, Owings & Merrill, and Minoru Yamasaki's design for the Reynolds Metals Building in Detroit, boasting a handsome aluminum screen wall, are fine architecture. There are outstanding instances also of research facilities, illustrated best by Saarinen's complex known as the General Motors Technical Center, in a great private park outside Detroit.

The design of manufacturing facilities is a different story, however. Early anonymous structures, like the great silos for the storage of wheat, had attracted the early modernists who saw them or, like Le Corbusier, knew them from photographs. Then there were important pioneering efforts by the architect Albert Kahn in the Detroit area early in the twentieth century (largely for the blossoming automobile industry), where he used concrete directly and sensibly before that structural material was common in the United States. There have been instances of outstanding design of factories since that time (even Frank Lloyd Wright got into this field with a well-known building for the Johnson's Wax Company in Racine, Wisconsin), but in most cases the typical factory building has been directly utilitarian, with an appendage for office space that often tries to be "architectural." Some of the great power plants, primarily the structures designed by Roland A. Wank, Harry B. Tour, and Rudolf J. Mock, architects for the Tennessee Valley Authority, are organized and articulated in an interesting architectural sense.

An advance that has been made in this area is the recent development of industrial "parks." In an attempt to relate industrial activity more pleasantly to the environment of the nearby community, landscaped and controlled groups of factories, better designed than most, have appeared from Massachusetts to California.

Fontana Dam (TVA), North Carolina
Architect: ROLAND WANK (TVA Staff)

5

RESIDENTIAL BUILDINGS

In the residential category, architects in the United States have produced many distinguished custom-designed and individually-built houses. There is a multitude of books to testify to this fact, and several very popular magazines find enough examples to fill their pages each month. Regional stylisms in residential design have very nearly passed from the national picture, and the early dominance of the Bay Area architects in California, or the New England group that centered around such talented local architects as Hugh A. Stubbins, Jr., Carl Koch, Robert Woods Kennedy in Massachuetts in the 1940's and 1950's, has given way to numerous individual styles and mannerisms, with little relation to region. Types range from the informal, rambling, earth-hugging design that derives partly from the Western ranch house and partly from Frank Lloyd Wright's organic approach, to the formal, often symmetrical design that can be traced to Mies van der Rohe and his early admirer, Philip Johnson, with many individual variations in between. One architect, John MacL. Johansen, in Connecticut, has been able in his own recent practice to pass through phases of rigid Palladian symmetry, sculptural free forms, and a design based on clustered, curved concrete piers. Some distinguished architects—Vienna-born Richard Neutra is outstanding among them—have abjured fantasy of this sort and continued producing well-planned and richly designed houses that vary only to suit conditions of the site.

A completely original, admittedly fantastic approach can be

seen in the work of Bruce Goff and his followers such as Herb
Green where curved forms, jutting angles and unusual materials including chunks of coal and glass, are used. Goff, influenced by Wright but a completely free and free-form spirit,
has taught at the University of Oklahoma and lives and practices now in Wright's Price Tower at Bartlesville.

Through all of the experiment where it exists and along with
the design accomplishment, one finds in the individual American home great progress in adaptable mechanical equipment,
in lighting and heating methods, and in insulation against the
weather. In fact, in the houses placed for sale in large residential developments, these comfortable modern mechanical additions are also common. The subdividers have not always been
careful in over-all planning, in preserving trees and green areas,
in making sure that schools or even roads are parts of the communities they are unwittingly building—although today there
is much more consciousness of these matters. By and large,

Architect's Own House, Westport, Connecticut
Architect: JOHN M. JOHANSEN

however, they have succeeded in building rapidly and relatively inexpensively, and including many amenities.

Not too many architects have been able to work in the atmosphere of rapid subdivision home building because the builders themselves, with an adaptation of the old wood balloon frame, can build more quickly when they are not hampered by "design" considerations. There are important exceptions, however. Architects such as Charles M. Goodman of Washington, D.C. and A. Quincy Jones, Jr., of Los Angeles, California, working with progressive and socially-minded builders such as Joseph Eichler of Palo Alto, California, have shown what can be done when building know-how and design skill join hands.

In another sort of housing, the problems of the high-rise building come into play again. The apartment house in the United States, like the individual speculative house, is often built by an entrepreneur who is primarily concerned with speed of erection and maximum number of square feet of rentable space. There are, therefore, not as many examples of first-rate architecture among the tall apartment houses as there are in the tall office building category. Nonetheless, fine instances do exist, ranging from the buildings by Mies van der Rohe on Michigan Avenue in Chicago (designed in his manner of clearly expressing the steel frame of the structure on the outside of the building, and using the largest possible amount of glass), to some by otherwise little-known firms, such as several new buildings in New York by architects Conklin & Whittlesey. Two buildings by this latter firm use exposed concrete in a manner that is direct, bold, and unusual in the northeast climate.

It can be said fairly that the unit planning of the individual apartment within the typical apartment building—the "house on a house on a house," as Louis Kahn defines it—is far superior to that in most of the industrialized countries. And again, the mechanical conveniences, from air conditioning to built-in dishwashers and wall-mounted ovens, are included as a matter of course.

As social planning became an accepted part of the philosophy of government in the United States in the 1930's, it was quickly recognized that the quantity and the quality of housing, whether in separate houses or in multi-family buildings, was inadequate for large parts of the population. High costs of construction and financing, as well as high land costs, had simply priced many worthy citizens out of the housing market. For these reasons it became necessary, as older housing deteriorated, as the population grew, and as costs for new buildings rose, to find ways of subsidizing public housing in order to reduce rents. It was difficult to reconcile low-cost rentals and high-quality design in public housing, although there are instances of good architectural solutions. Some, such as a project by John Carl Warnecke & Associates in California, have even drawn criticism from the economy minded because they were "too good," even though their costs were in reality no higher than less well designed examples. Recently, the Public Housing Administration in Washington has determined to improve architectural quality, and the advice of excellent architects has been sought in various parts of the country. Perhaps soon this category can be commended as highly for its architectural accomplishments as for its social purposes.

6.

BUILDINGS FOR PUBLIC USE

Recently a category of buildings that had seemed bogged in conservatism has shown signs of remarkable design activity. Public buildings, sponsored by government agencies, are beginning to attract the attention of talented architects. An outstanding instance has been the program of the State Department to build embassies and other official United States headquarters buildings in foreign lands. Many of the finest of the young as

U.S. Embassy, New Delhi, India
Architect: Edward D. Stone

well as the mature architects have been drawn into this program, and the structures they have designed have related well to the countries in which they were built. Edward Durell Stone's embassy in New Delhi, India, that of Walter Gropius's group in Athens, the design of Jose Luis Sert for Baghdad, and others, have made government agencies realize that not all federal projects—or even state- or city-sponsored work—need be stodgy, nor cast in the conventional semimodern mold that has tended to prevail until recently.

More and more, good design has appeared in such buildings as local post offices, city halls (as the design for Boston, for which a competition was held) and arts centers (as one in Memphis, Tennessee, designed by the young firm of Mann & Harrover, also as the result of a competition). Among quasi-government structures, the Lincoln Center for the Performing Arts in New York must be noted. There, a number of architects —Wallace Harrison, Max Abramovitz, Pietro Belluschi, Philip Johnson, Gordon Bunshaft, Eero Saarinen—have worked to-

Arena Stage Theater, Washington, D.C.
Architect: HARRY WEESE

gether somewhat as a team, designing separate buildings, to produce a dignified (some critics think almost pompous) group of buildings. In other cities also, interesting theaters and concert halls and similar structures of a community nature have been built. An outstanding instance is the Arena Stage in Washington, D.C., by a Chicago architect, Harry M. Weese, whose sensitive designs are much admired by his fellow architects.

Two types of institutional building—that is, closely related to over-all community life—have received much attention in recent years, and have shown great advance in adaptability to modern human needs. They are buildings for health care and those for educational purposes.

It has been noted that during the pre-war period, the United States government adopted a program of hospital construction, recognizing the needs of the individual states but requiring certain standards to warrant federal financial assistance. One result of this was the study, by a devoted group of civil service architects, of all of the complicated functions of hospital care. One such person was Marshall Shaffer, whose work has already been noted. Another was Isadore Rosenfield, a serious student of hospital design problems and a writer on the subject, who at one time was chief hospital architect for the City of New York and has since conducted his own practice.

As a result of these studies, an almost stereotyped hospital plan, relating carefully the functional relationships of such elements as the nursing unit where the patient in the hospital is cared for, the operating suite, the central storage and sterilization facilities, and the out-patient clinics where ambulant patients who come from their homes receive attention, has been built with individual variations all over the United States.

Recently, new nursing techniques have caused a re-study of this often repeated plan, and several architects have devoted themselves to the problem of humanizing further both the internal arrangement and the plastic form of the building.

Schools have occupied the design attention of a large number of capable architects in recent years. At the end of the war, the great need was for elementary schools. As population ages changed, facilities for teaching children in high school were needed more and more, and what came to be called the K-12 school problem (kindergarten through high school) brought much study. Now the college and university needs are very great, and are being partially met by a new, intermediate, sometimes terminal, institution—the junior college. Many of the architectural firms that began their practices after the war started in the school field. John Lyon Reid, in San Francisco, has for several decades been seriously studying the translation of educational programs into flexible and handsome buildings. William W. Caudill, a Texas architect and educator always interested in research, has done much experiment in plan and in technology. Lawrence B. Perkins and Philip Will, Jr., in Chicago have carried on from their early contemporary school at Crow Island in Illinois to a large and successful practice. Ernest J. Kump, another Californian, has moved from distinguished elementary school solutions (with experiments in prefabrication at one time) to junior college problems, and his concrete and redwood Foothill College has been much admired.

There have been studies in lighting, in classroom arrangement, in circulation, in the use of new, audio-visual equipment. The large city school, occupying costly urban land, has not always been successful in meeting new requirements with new, interesting forms. More than in the outlying areas, school boards in the urban centers generally tend to be conservative, even in the face of changing methods of instruction (such as group teaching, and the use of mechanical teaching aids) and of changing architectural attitudes.

A few breaks in this wall of resistance have resulted in remarkable achievements, however. For a time in New Orleans, Louisiana, for example, the work of Charles R. Colbert (another of the devoted practitioners who have given time to education for architecture), and that of several other firms such as Curtis & Davis, became widely recognized. Another instance is the group of schools that were erected in Sarasota, Florida, by Paul Rudolph, Victor Lundy and others, under the encouraging guidance of a school board headed by an architecture-minded chairman—Philip Hiss—whose advice is now sought by other school planning groups.

It took a longer time for the traditional collegiate-gothic college campus to open its arms and the minds of its trustees to contemporary moves in architecture. Only in very recent years, under pressure of great expansion, have some of the older campuses added new buildings with true architectural merit. At Harvard, Gropius, with his firm, the Architects' Collaborative broke the ice during his tenure of Design, by designing a Graduate Center at the school where he used sculpture, painting, and ceramics by some of his former Bauhaus colleagues. In more recent years at that institution, Jose Luis Sert, the present dean, Hugh Stubbins, an architect who is perhaps best known for his Conference Hall built in Berlin for the Exposition of 1955, and others have added interesting buildings. The most recent is a new Fine Arts Center by the French architect, Le Corbusier—his first work in the United States aside from his part in the design of United Nations headquarters, and a building admired for its strength but criticized for its unharmonious relationship to its surroundings.

M. I. T., with several buildings by Saarinen, an almost brutal brick dormitory with a sculptural outside stair by the great Finnish architect Alvar Aalto, and a recent high-rise building by Pei has also broken with tradition. Yale University has an exhibition of almost unrelated semi-masterpieces by Paul Rudolph (head of the department of architecture there), Gordon Bunshaft and Philip Johnson, with a recent pair of new residential colleges designed by Eero Saarinen in a romantic, almost neo-Gothic manner. The University of Pennsylvania boasts Louis

Carpenter Center for the Visual Arts, Harvard University
Cambridge, Massachusetts
Architect: LE CORBUSIER

Kahn's Richards Medical Research building and a dormitory by Saarinen. On most of the older campuses, however, the new buildings have either been reminiscent (as at Princeton), timid (a tendency of which Columbia University is an instance), or diverse (as the campus of the University of California at Berkeley, where fortunately the great trees and the landscaping of Thomas Church bring the varied new buildings into a unity).

It is the totally new campus, unhampered by tradition and perhaps ready to pursue a new educational concept, that holds the promise of really distinguished architecture in this field.

McGregor Memorial Conference Center, Wayne University, Detroit, Michigan
Architect: MINORU YAMASAKI

The architects who are concerned with the problem find themselves becoming land planners as well as designers of buildings. Many of the new campuses, such as the extensions of the University of California at Santa Cruz, for which John Carl Warnecke and Associates are master-plan architects, with Anshen & Allen, Theodore Bernardi, and Ernest Kump as consulting architects; or at Irvine, California, where William Pereira is planning and designing; or San Diego, the job of Robert E. Alexander, each of which is planned for an ultimate 27,500 students, pose problems of building relationship comparable only to the laying out of a city.

7

LARGE-SCALE DESIGN

In the design of a large university campus, as we have seen, in the design of a shopping center with all of its concomitant elements, in the design of an industrial park with its necessary connections to adjacent community facilities and transportations, and in many other cases as well, the architect in the United States today finds himself drawn more and more to problems of large-scale relationships of a sort that only city planners faced in the past. America is growing not by single building increments, but by groups of related buildings, by segments of cities, and by the addition of complete new towns to the expanding metropolitan areas. The architect indeed finds himself becoming a planner. Questions of the nature of a city, the proper method of growth, the replacement of blighted and worn-out sections, and the interconnections between the areas of intensive use, are passing from the realm of theoretical speculation to actual commissions that must be solved.

This impingement of city planning problems on architecture has had two effects: the first, obviously, was to bring new social planning questions forward for discussion; the second has been to alter sharply the nature of the practice of architecture. As a result of the first impact, a vigorous and healthy debate has resulted. In print, literature on the subject has ranged from the rather sentimental and romantic appeal by Jane Jacobs for natural growth of the city and retention of its older characteristics in her book, *The Death and Life of Great American Cities*, to the more scholarly findings of Kevin Lynch. In his book, *The*

Image of the City, he developed the thesis that inhabitants of a city need strong visual notions and recollections of the places within which they move about. The bitter findings of Lewis Mumford, in *The City in History*—that Megalopolis, the vast, continuous city, is a pretty discouraging place in a cultural sense—should also be mentioned. More to the point, perhaps, are research studies such as those carried on jointly by Harvard and M. I. T. under the direction of Martin Myerson, or by the Center for Metropolitan Studies in Washington, D.C., under the leadership of Frederick Gutheim. In these studies is being laid the basis for the planning that must come, as the American city expands beyond its present borders, or as the remaining spaces between city centers is filled even more, or as the older central portions are torn down and rebuilt.

It is this last step, actually, that has come first, because the needs were most pressing. The federal government for some years has sponsored projects and allocated funds to cities that proceeded with organized redevelopment plans under the direction of their own local authorities. The money has been used primarily to devalue over-valued land and allow its re-use for either residential or commercial purposes. Many of these projects are under way, in New York, Philadelphia, St. Louis, San Francisco, and many other cities, and although the results to date have sometimes been criticized as too broad and insufficiently humanized planning, much work that is praiseworthy and some that is brilliant has been started. The devotion of public officials and architects to the problems of redevelopment promises more advance in this direction in the future.

Actual new-city building—starting a new community from scratch, on a scale larger than a subdivision—has been rare since pioneer days. Some of the new towns that have been mentioned as planned during the 1930's are almost the only exceptions. But recognizing the fact that the great spaces between,

for instance, the string of cities along the eastern seaboard—
Boston, New York, Philadelphia, Baltimore, Washington, and
Richmond—were being filled in willy-nilly in a chaotic fashion,
planners are now concerned with directing these intercity connections into planned, related communities.

The Year 2000 Plan for Washington, D.C., prepared by the
National Capital Planning Commission and the National Capital Regional Planning Council is an outstanding instance of
such planning. It is based on a belief that carefully placed new
towns along networks of communications and transportation
facilities radiating out from the central city will form a logical
method of growth. Planning theories range today from a desire
to plan in an organized manner such as this, to the opposite
extreme—a satisfaction with "planned sprawl" (some mini-
mum degree of control over the natural expansion of a city) as
an evidence of organic growth. Since theories vary so greatly,
the Washington Plan has been both praised and criticized.
Since even basic social theories can include a belief that man
needs relief from the city, or the seemingly contradictory conviction that we are inevitably becoming a completely urban
society, disagreement on published plans is understandable and
will surely continue. Nonetheless, the Washington Plan is already resulting in the beginning of new communities in the
area, such as Reston, in Virginia, planned by architects Conklin
and Whittlesey. This and other planning efforts will produce
in the next few years the first new towns to be built in the
United States since Clarence Stein's Radburn, New Jersey, in
the 1930's.

8.

CHANGING PRACTICE

Another effect of the concern with planning is that the architect today is being forced to extend his practice beyond single-building design into the design of groups of buildings—as we have seen, into city planning. It is more and more common to find the letterhead of an archiect describing him as "architect and planner," or "architect and planning consultant." There is an increasing professional education of planners as such, and several professional associations represent this separate discipline. However, the planner is likely to be concerned primarily with research statistics and regulations, while the architect-planner is leading his studies always to the three-dimensional architectural results. A distinction has thus been made between "urban planning" and "urban design." The American Institute of Architects is launched on a firm campaign to convince its members of the necessity of "comprehensive practice," which includes, among other new responsibilities, an understanding of and an ability in broad-scale planning.

The other responsibilities included in the "comprehensive" concept of architectural practice are greater knowledge of the financing and land assembly aspects of the building process. Much of this change in architecture results from a changing sort of client. The architect in the United States is not likely to be designing today for an individual, as did the Colonial, the Federal, or the post- and pre-Civil War architects. He is much more likely to count as his clients government agencies, school boards, church building committees, corporate boards of directors, or entrepreneurs and land developers who are also answerable to directors and stock holders. It is very much to his credit that he has been able to adapt to that change, realize the needs for thinking in larger terms than the single unit for the single client, and create the number of instances of outstanding architecture that have been reviewed so very quickly in this book.

CONCLUSION

At any time in history, the number of truly creative people is a small part of the total population, and the number of great achievements in architecture, as in any of the other arts, is also small. It is remarkable that so many structures of genuine worth, that are likely to endure in the histories of world architecture, have been designed and built in the short life of the United States. America is still continuing its explosive growth, begun in Colonial times, and its history remains a dynamic one. The very vigor of its expansion seems to have provided a sympathetic environment for creative architectural accomplishment —both by native-born architects and by those who have come to its shores from other, older lands.

American architecture is more than a synthesis of designs conceived in other times and other places, and yet it has built proudly on the backgrounds of its people. Whether their ancestry was English and the architecture they drew from was that of the late middle ages and the Renaissance, as in the beginning; or French and *Beaux Arts* influenced, as later; or middle European and inspired by the excitement of the early modern movement in the arts—in continuing, successive numbers, architects from the Old World have arrived and transfused the talent that was developing in the new country.

Never has the fusion of backgrounds been more clear or more effective than at the present moment. Consider first some names that have been mentioned in these pages: Belluschi, Breuer, Gropius, Gruen, Kiesler, Lescaze, Neutra, Pei, Saarinen, Sert, van der Rohe, Yamasaki. These and many others have enriched an architecture that could also draw on the work of those whose ancestry was longer in the United States—people such as Richardson, Hunt, Sullivan, Maybeck, Goodhue, Wright. And yet, to carry the point further, even the "native" architecture in the United States has often had a strong influence from other places. Wright and Maybeck, each in his own way, were influenced by design from the Orient; Hunt and Richardson were romantically aware of the medieval periods of Western Europe.

This is not to say, however, that architecture in the United States has been uniformly eclectic or merely a synthesis. The excitement that it produces in those who see it today, and the influence it is having on other lands, in its turn, could come about only through originality and creative strength. Something has been added to what was there in the beginning. The great addition, probably, has been technological accomplishment. Methods of engineering design and techniques of construction have been developed rapidly and efficiently. In addition, there has been a refining process on the one hand (Mies's glass-walled office building is surely a refinement of his earlier, European work), and an infusion of boldness on the other hand (the audacity of Eero Saarinen's forms are an interesting contrast to the urbane modernism of his father's work).

As a picture of its society, then, architecture in the United States reflects a land into which have flowed many streams of creative development, and where they have all been gathered together into a strong, forward-moving current. Today it is a picture of growth, vigor, imagination, and an ability strong enough to direct the current to new ends—new social goals, new esthetic principles, new technological possibilities.

GLOSSARY

Adobe. A brick or building material made of sun-dried earth with straw binder.

Base. The lower part of a wall, pier or column, considered as a separate architectural feature.

Beam. A horizontal weight-supporting member of a structural frame.

Capital (or *cap*). In a classical column, the top part, often forming a transition between the column shaft and a horizontal beam above.

Column. A vertical weight-supporting member of a structural frame. Classically, a column generally consists of base, a usually cylindrical shaft, and a capital. In contemporary terms, it may be without variation from top to bottom.

Corner, (in-cut, cut-off, notched, etc.) In contemporary architecture, one of various attempts to indicate visually a new structural freedom, in this instance by eliminating the traditional corner support of a structure.

Cornice. A projecting and often molded horizontal member at the top of the wall.

Eave. The lower edge of a roof that projects out over a wall.

Foliated. Shaped like a leaf or group of leaves.

Gable. The upper triangular end of a wall, in a building with a sloping roof.

Gambrel. A roof whose ends are cut off on a vertical plane and whose sides have two slopes, the lower one being the steeper.

Gallery. Space formed by inserting in an enclosed area a partial intermediate floor that projects out from one or more walls.

Girder. A main horizontal weight-supporting member of a structural frame, usually supporting secondary beams.

Gridiron. An arrangement of streets resembling a utensil of parallel metal bars; i.e., straight streets, parallel to one another.

Infill. Material forming a wall between separated supporting vertical members, as masonry between timbers in half-timber construction, or as curtain-wall panels between steel or concrete columns.

Masonry. Stonework.

Mullion. A vertical division member between windows, doors, screens, etc. in a series.

Overhang. The projection of a member beyond the face below it; specifically, an upper story or a roof projecting some distance beyond its supporting wall.

Pier. An upright structural member, usually of masonry, serving as a principal support.

Planes. Flat surfaces.

Prefabricated. Descriptive of a method of construction where elements up to the size of a total house are manufactured in standardized units before arrival at the building site.

Pueblo. A flat-roofed stone or adobe house or aggregation of houses, used as a communal dwelling by Indians in the southwest U.S.A.

Rafter. A sloping structural member of a roof frame, beneath and supporting the roofing material or roof boards.

Ramp. A sloping surface in the nature of a floor, joining different levels of a structure.

Ridge. The top horizontal member of a sloping roof, against which the ends of the rafters are fixed.

Shaft. That portion of a classical column between the capital and the base.

Sill. The lower horizontal member of a structural framing system, usually supported by the foundation, and in its turn bearing the vertical framing members.

Stucco. A material usually made of portland cement, sand and some lime, applied in a plastic state to form a hard covering for exterior walls.

Teepee. American Indian tent, cone-shaped made of skins, supported by wooden poles.

Terra-cotta. Cast and fired clay, in units usually larger than bricks, that can be used for surfacing of a building.

Truss. An assemblage of straight structural members forming a rigid, web-like framework to provide beam action over long spans or to support unusually heavy loads.

SUGGESTIONS FOR FURTHER READING

1. Banham, Reyner, *Guide to Modern Architecture,* Van Nostrand, 1963
2. Blake, Peter, *The Master Builders,* Knopf, 1960
3. Burchard, John, and Bush Brown, Albert, *The Architecture of America,* Little-Brown, 1961
4. Churchill, Henry, *The City Is the People,* Norton, 1962
5. Fitch, James M., *American Building,* Houghton Mifflin, 1948
6. Goodman, Percival and Paul, *Communitas,* Vintage, 1960*
7. Hitchcock, Henry-Russell, *Architecture Nineteen and Twentieth Centuries,* Penguin, 1958*
8. Morrison, Hugh, *Louis Sullivan,* Norton, 1935
9. Mumford, Lewis, *The Brown Decades,* Dover, 1955*
10. Mumford, Lewis, *Roots of American Architecture,* Evergreen, 1958*
11. Mumford, Lewis, *Sticks and Stones,* Dover, 1955*
12. Richards, J. M., *An Introduction to Modern Architecture,* Penguin, 1947*
13. Sullivan, Lewis, *Autobiography of an Idea,* Dover, 1956*
14. Tunnard, Christopher and Reed, Henry Hope, Jr., *American Skyline,* Mentor, 1953*
15. Wright, Frank Lloyd, *Future of Architecture,* Mentor, 1956*
16. Wright, Frank Lloyd, *Writings and Buildings,* selected by Kaufmann, Edgar and Raeburn, Ben, Meridian, 1960*

* Paperbound

THE AUTHOR

THOMAS H. CREIGHTON is both a practicing architect and a writer on architectural subjects. Currently a partner in the noted San Francisco firm of John Carl Warnecke & Associates, he is a former editor of the magazine *Progressive Architecture,* and author of numerous books, including *Building for Modern Man, Contemporary Houses, the American House Today,* and *Architecture of Monuments.*

PAUL SPREIREGEN, who is widely known for his architectural drawings, is Head of Urban Design Projects at the American Institute of Architects in Washington, D.C.